ISBN 1-85437-034-0

Published by order of the Trustees 1990 for the collection display 20 February 1990 – 13 January 1991.

Selected by Richard Francis
Exhibitions Assistant Jemima Pyne
Prepared by Tate Gallery Liverpool, Albert Dock, Liverpool L3 4BB.
Designed by Jeremy Greenwood
Colour origination by Axis Photo Litho, Runcorn
Printed in Great Britain by Cox Rockliff Limited, Liverpool.

Illustration credits

Tate Gallery Publications for all works in Tate Collection
Arts Council Collection, South Bank Centre, London
Marlborough Fine Art
Private Collection, Switzerland

Cover

*Seated Figure*, 1974

# FRANCIS BACON

TATE GALLERY LIVERPOOL

# PREFACE

Francis Bacon, regarded by many as Britain's foremost twentieth century painter, is certainly a great European artist. His antecedents in painting, philosophy and literature are those intellectuals who have helped form our view not only of art but of the world as a whole. The view that he gives us may, on occasions, frighten us as it refuses to ignore the anxieties of this century. It is a modern view in every sense.

The Tate has had a long association with Bacon having presented major retrospectives in 1962 and 1985. We are fortunate to have collected his work for 45 years and to have important examples from all periods. On this occasion we have enhanced our holdings with loans from private collections in Switzerland, England and the Arts Council Collection and hope very much to include some of the artist's most recent work.

We have been helped as usual by the great kindness of Valerie Beston at Marlborough Fine Art.

Nicholas Serota
Director, Tate Gallery

Richard Francis
Curator, Tate Gallery Liverpool

*Study of a Dog*, 1952

# MEMORY TRACES

Richard Francis

Francis Bacon urges us to his paintings, to look at them closely and discover how they are made rather than uncover the story of why they are made. He does not wish us to enquire for example who the paintings depict, why or when; their history in relation to his biography is avoided; the titles lack emotional content and are descriptive of types (Study, Triptych, Portrait) rather than occasions. If we know the way in which Bacon combines images and ideas it may help us to approach the work but it rarely reveals the artist's emotions and the context of his enquiry. He 'speaks of' his work in the extraordinary series of interviews with David Sylvester and occasionally reveals part of himself, but it is as if he is presenting his thoughts to us, in the way he displays the paintings, behind a unifying glass and within a strict and aristocratic frame.

We are encouraged by him to return to the paintings themselves and to their surfaces, to consider 'chance' procedures, thrown paint, impressions of cloth or objects, images developed unconsciously, accidentally or appropriated from photographs. Andrew Durham talks eloquently of this in his technical note. The information is significant but insufficiently revelatory. Our attention to the method of making may reveal clues about the artist's attitude to the world but it does not unlock the meaning of the works in front of us.

In fact looking at the works is closer to our experience of the world outside art than to the relatively restricted experience we have in galleries. His works convey the sense of charged moments and actions and we recognise an extraordinary vitality. Like our participation in events the emotions are intense and, as we experience them, we may be in a state of suspended judgment. Being there almost guarantees that the gruesome and horrific are disregarded in the heat of the moment. Bacon's work aspires to this condition, to the status of reported or recorded real-life. The real world is played up whilst precedents in painting or ideas of modern art are played down. Thus Bacon may acknowledge the significance of Picasso's 1928 paintings but he disregards them in his primary wish 'to return the onlooker to life more violently'. This is not only a wish to explore the visceral but to distance himself from what he regards as the intellectual and aesthetic inadequacy of much modern abstract art. His art is about the human condition and he wants his 'pictures to look as if a human being had passed between them, like a snail, leaving a trail of the human presence and a memory trace of past events'.[1]

He has talked on several occasions of the images of his paintings coming to him during daydreams, when 'pictures fall in just like slides'[2] and of these images being the start of the process of making the picture. The process begins with recollection and is made active through the chancy

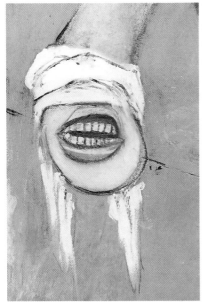

business of painting. Bacon encourages accidents whilst making the images in order to produce a deeper memory of the event. The encouraged accident may produce forms and shapes that trigger in the artist and the spectator heightened emotional responses, 'I think the whole process of this sort of elliptical form is dependent on the execution of detail and how shapes are remade or put out of focus to bring in their memory traces'.[3] Almost unapproachable events, depicted in paintings of the Crucifixion and secular subjects, for instance a screaming head, of necessity provoke the strongest reactions. (Consider Bacon's 'Study for Three Figures at the Base of a Crucifixion' where the forms of the bodies have an extraordinary tenderness, repeated many times in the next forty years, and where the screaming mouth begins a process of unlocking areas inaccessible to conventional thought.)

Given this ambition Bacon could not be satisfied with abstraction; he needs the human as subject and his art must be representational rather than allude through abstract forms or symbolic substitutes. The precedents he chooses, therefore, to discuss are from earlier masters. For each he has an unconventional justification, Poussin for the scream, Rembrandt for the extraordinary use of paint in an eye socket, Ingres for his ability to express through elegant distortion, Degas for the way in which the bones appear under the flesh. These are the masters that Bacon acknowledges; there are others that we might wish to add but he regards them as unimportant. What distinguishes Bacon's work from all of them (his list and ours) is its modernity. The work exists now because it acknowledges that the conventions of picture making have been irrevocably changed by photography and film (the 'modern' medium) and because it examines its own attitudes and behaviour. It represents the world in terms of its own ideas rather than representing a convention (which is what we assume, perhaps wrongly, about earlier art). Bacon's art appears to represent the extremity of the moment, and the screens that he uses to convert it for us from the world to the canvas are at times almost transparent. This is, for me, the essence of his modernity and what distinguishes him from his earlier canon of artists.

It is a modernity expressed in ideas and has its roots in the intellectual history of the modern arts. Baudelaire's essay *The Painter of Modern Life* sets the agenda, viz 'The artist, man of the world, man of the crowd, and child' and begins: 'Today I want to discourse to the public about a strange man, a man of so powerful and so decided an originality that it is sufficient unto itself and does not even seek approval . . . all his works are signed – with his dazzling *soul*'.[4]

Baudelaire postulates that the artist at his most receptive is in the condition of the convalescent, and that this is also close to the most impressionable period of his childhood. He declares that 'genius is nothing more than *childhood recovered* at will' and defines the artist's eternal receptivity. He goes on to describe the artist as *'Flâneur'*, 'a passionate spectator', raises him above 'the fugitive pleasure of circumstances' and has him looking for 'modernity' itself. He makes it his business to extract from fashion whatever element it may contain of poetry within history, to

Details, *Three Studies for Figures at the Base of a Crucifixion,* c1944 distil the eternal from the transitory.[5] His hero, the modern man, stands outside the society he is describing and is a modern aristocrat, the dandy who by adopting the modernist stance and transforming the instant becomes the modern hero.

The intellectual tradition of this modernist position run through much 20th century philosophy and is apparent in Nietzsche, Proust and Freud. They have taken the Baudelairean project and exemplified it throughout their work. Each uses these principles to extend and explain their world; each uses memory and reconstruction of the instantaneous to organise their own particular vulnerability. Freud distinguishes between recollection and memory. The former is our normal process of incorporating and reconciling our experience of the world; it is usually a conscious and a conservative (in the sense of 'taking care of') process.

Memory is destructive since it is most powerful when it remains hidden from our conscious mind and appears to us unresolved in our unexplained actions. Bacon, like Proust is striving to make himself and us aware of these 'memory traces' and excites himself to provoke their reception on his canvases. Perhaps this is his subject matter, the concern to discover our hidden memory and to stimulate its approximation in paint. It is a dangerous activity in which the artist risks his own creativity as he tries to recapture not the recollection of the moment (a Romantic notion) but the memory trace (a Heroic notion) from within his unconscious.

Heroic it may be in Modernist terms, but it is inevitably futile and its meanings come only in the act of creating those meanings. Bacon speaks in the interviews of 'giving this purposeless existence a meaning by our drives . . . I do think that, if you can find a person totally without belief, but totally dedicated to futility, then you will find the more exciting person'.[6] Those drives by which we measure our lives provide us too with a measure of our understanding of modern painting and poetry and enable us to recognise, if not make, significant descriptions of the world. Like Eliot's crowd flowing over London Bridge ('I had not thought death had undone so many') we may recognise our companions, if we are fortunate, on the road. 'You! – hypocrite lecteur! – mon semblable, – mon frère!'[7]

NOTES

1. Francis Bacon [statement], *The New Decade: 22 European Painters and Sculptors*, exh. cat., May-Aug 1955, Museum of Modern Art, New York

2. David Sylvester, *Interviews with Francis Bacon*, London, new and enlarged edition 1980

3. *The New Decade: 22 European Painters and Sculptors*

4. Baudelaire, *The Painter of Modern Life and Other Essays*, translated and edited by Jonathan Mayne, London, 1964, p 5

5. *ibid.*

6. *Interviews with Francis Bacon*, p 134

7. T S Eliot, *The Waste Land* from *Collected Poems 1909-62*, London, 1963, p 65

# NOTE ON TECHNIQUE

Andrew Durham

Bacon can by no means be called a conventional artist; he can no more be called a conventional painter. Nevertheless his range of materials is extremely limited and he restricts himself rigorously to painting. The importance to him of photography, for example, seems to have been the subsequent liberation of the painter to exploit the properties of paint without regard to narration or description, rather than his own involvement in any photographic procedures.

The 'Three Studies for Figures at the Base of a Crucifixion' were painted on Sundeala board, a light and absorbent wood-fibre board, then commonly used by artists; Roy de Maistre and Graham Sutherland, both close friends of Bacon, were using Sundeala as a support at the time. But this use was dictated by economic expediency rather than considered choice. Although Sundeala had its advantages (in Bacon's opinion 'it held pastel well'), he changed to using canvas as soon as he could afford to. Initially he used the canvas in the usual way, painting on the commercially prepared priming. It was not an ideal surface, however; pastel did not adhere well but more importantly it did not have sufficient 'tooth' to receive the pastel or the paint in the way he wanted. It was by accident, having run out of material, and painting on the back of an already used canvas in 1947-8, that he discovered the absorbent, unprimed surface which has since become his standard support. For the last twenty or thirty years he has used ready-primed canvases stretched back to front from the same artists' colourman. Bacon does not size the canvas before beginning the picture, nor does he make a preparatory drawing.

Most of his painting is done with a brush; 'he draws with the brush'. He always begins with the central image, the frenetic brushstrokes contrasting with the more sedately executed background areas, which are added and adapted as the image as a whole progresses. He may not always work fast and furiously, but the paintings he regards as the more successful are in general the ones he paints quickly.

With the brush Bacon achieves an extraordinary variety of effects. These range from calligraphic arabesques, through sharp stabbing strokes to the almost watercolourist's delicacy of the treatment of the hair in the right-hand figure of 'Triptych – August 1972' (p 22), to voluptuous impasto with a heavily laden brush, and the dragging of dry paint across the surface to leave encrustations rather than brushstrokes. Elsewhere he picks the brush off the surface to leave sharp peaks and serrated ridges of paint.

For the painting of the image Bacon uses predominantly, but not exclusively, artists' oil colour. He does not add extra oil or any other medium such as varnish. He does add a diluent – usually turpentine. The nature of the applied paint varies from thick dollops squeezed directly on to the canvas from the tube, high impasto and dry scumbles where the medium seems to have been soaked out, to very thin washes where a good deal of turpentine has been added to modify the tube paint. He seems to delight in the subtlety and malleability of this medium.

He will alter the properties of the paint still further, to achieve the effect he wants. He adds sand to it while wet, as in the centre panel of 'Triptych – August 1972' where it is used to enhance the jagged impasto of the sweeping white brushstroke and also to modify the subtle modelling of the back. He leaves cotton wool and canvas fibres jutting out of the paint, and sometimes rubs his fingers along a dusty surface in the studio and then into the wet paint.

Bacon also manipulates the paint with his fingers, exploiting its malleable plasticity or smearing and smudging thin washes. Sometimes squashing blobs of paint with his thumb. He uses a rag or a sponge to push and distort outlines and surfaces, the result being a controlled accident, or imposes an almost disciplined 'cross-hatching' by pressing a piece of corduroy against the face in a portrait. He sometimes scrubs the canvas so the fibres of the threads are broken and jutting, then sprays them with an aerosol. Bacon adapts and enhances the image with highlights of pastel and achieves amorphous, cloud-like effects by spraying aerosol car paints over the image. He flicks or spatters paint onto the canvas, leaving it to run and drip. He may throw or rub sand into the paint or start by throwing the paint at the canvas in the hope that the image will create itself. The least painterly material he uses, and the closest he comes to the unpainterly medium of collage, is Letraset. It is applied in his customary, chance way and not with the precision of the graphic artist.

In talking of his work, Bacon draws a sharp distinction between the central image and the background. This distinction is reflected in the materials he uses. For the background he uses acrylic paints; they can be applied quickly and smoothly but are 'not subtle enough' for the central image. He also uses emulsion house paints which, like artists' acrylics, are fast-drying and convenient for the large expanses of flat colour. This is not to say, however, that the background is completed and the image then superimposed upon it. The background, while 'only a back to the image' is nevertheless a crucial and integral part of the whole and in terms of sequence it is modified and developed as the painting progresses.

He does not varnish the paintings when finished nor does he use intermediary layers of varnish during painting. The contrast between matt and gloss areas is a major aspect of the image, but Bacon maintains that this is also a result of chance.

It is clear that within the context of his working practices, the selective critical process whereby he adapts the accidents of his creative acts cannot be separated from the acts themselves either sequentially or emotively. Chance is exploited but the result is far from arbitrary: 'the creative and the critical become a single act'.

*Study for a Portrait of Van Gogh, 1957*

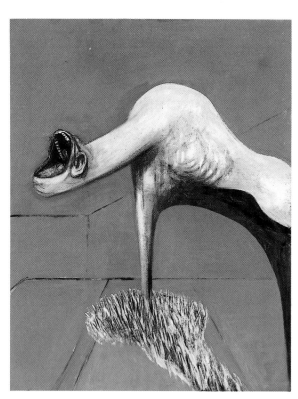

*Three Studies for Figures at the Base of a
Crucifixion, c1944*

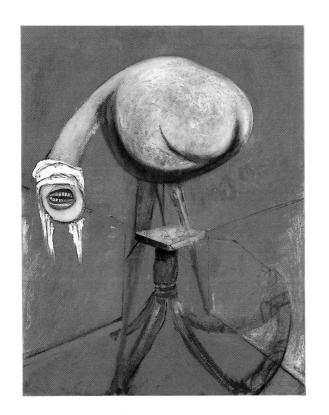

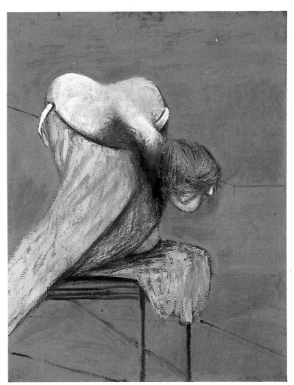

*Reclining Woman*, 1961

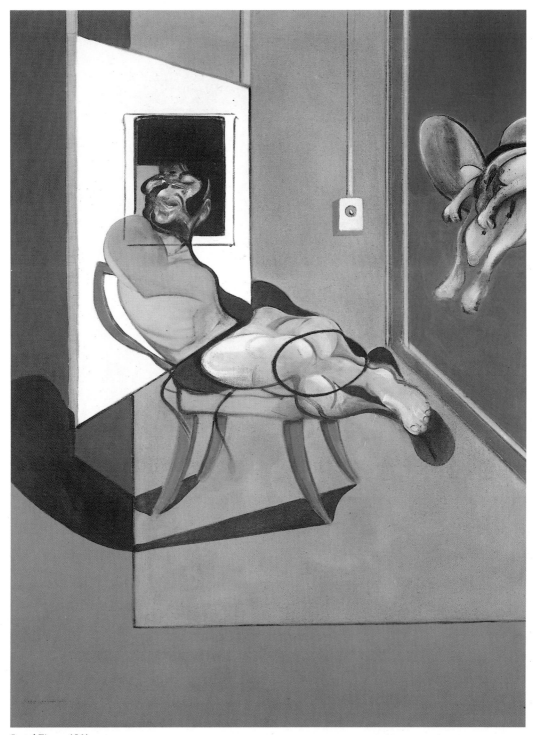

*Seated Figure*, 1961

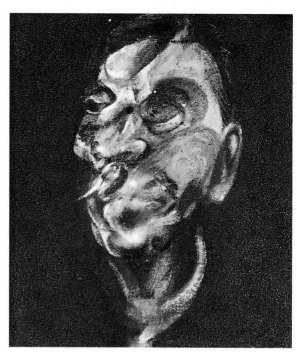

*Three Studies for Portrait of George Dyer, 1963*

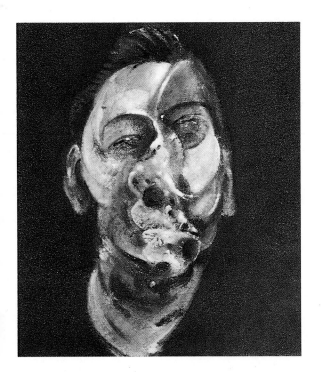 

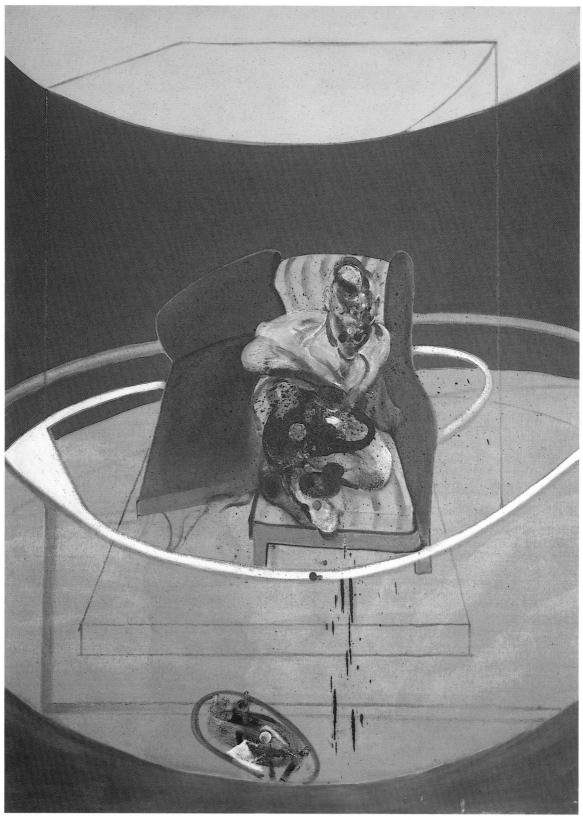

*Study for Portrait on a Folding Bed*, 1963

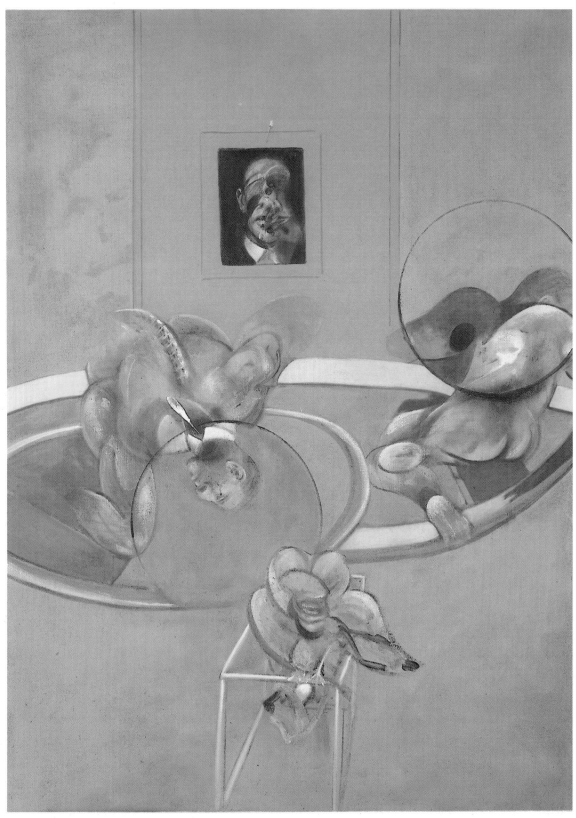

*Three Figures and Portrait*, 1975

*Triptych – August 1972, 1972*

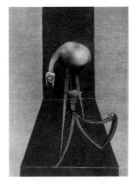

*Second Version Triptych 1944,* 1988, the artist
(not in display)

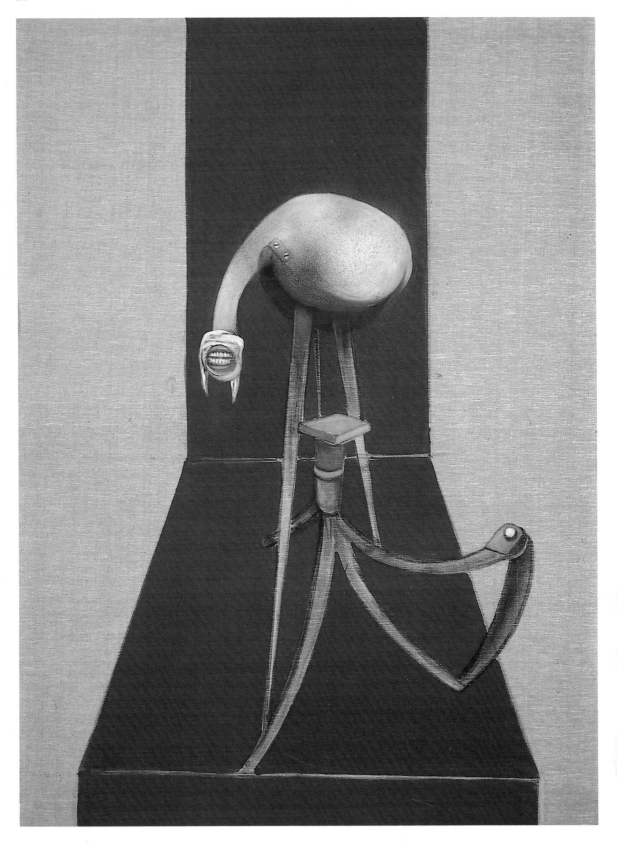

# LIST OF WORKS IN THE DISPLAY

FRANCIS BACON
born 1909

*Three Studies for Figures at the Base of a Crucifixion* c1944
Oil on Sundeala hardboard
Three panels, each 940 x 737mm
Presented by Mr E Hall 1952
N06171, N06172, N06173

*Figure in a Landscape* 1945
Oil on canvas
1448 x 1283 mm
Purchased 1950
N05941
(from September 1990)

*Study of a Dog* 1952
Oil on canvas
1981 x 1372mm
Presented by Mr E Hall 1952
N06131

*Study for a Portrait of Van Gogh* 1957
Oil on canvas
1981 x 1422 mm
Arts Council Collection, South Bank
Centre, London

*Reclining Woman* 1961
Oil and collage on canvas
1988 x 1416mm
Purchased 1961
T00453

*Seated Figure* 1961
Oil on canvas
1651 x 1422mm
Presented by J Sainsbury Ltd 1961
T00459

*Study for Portrait on Folding Bed* 1963
Oil on canvas
1981 x 1473
Purchased 1963
T00604

*Three Studies for a Portrait of George Dyer* 1963
Oil on canvas
Three panels, each 355 x 305mm
Private Collection

*Three Figures and Portrait,* d1975
Oil and pastel on canvas
1981 x 1473mm
Purchased 1977
T02112

*Triptych – August 1972* 1972
Oil on canvas
Three panels, each 1981 x 1473mm
Purchased 1980
T03073

*Seated Figure* 1974
Oil and pastel on canvas
1980 x 1475 mm
Private Collection, Switzerland

# SELECT BIBLIOGRAPHY

Extracted from a bibliography compiled by Krzysztof Ciewzkowski in 1984 for the Tate Gallery one-man catalogue.

This bibliography excludes most of the interviews with the artist, all sections of books, articles and reviews and group exhibition catalogues. It includes major one-man exhibitions in public galleries.

## 1 BOOKS

Alley, Ronald, and John Rothenstein, *Francis Bacon* (introd. by John Rothenstein, text by Ronald Alley), London, Thames and Hudson; New York, Viking Press, 1964.

Davies, Hugh Marlais, *Francis Bacon: The Early and Middle Years. 1928-1958* (PhD dissertation, Princeton University, Department of Art and Archaeology, Aug. 1975), New York, London, Garland Publishing, 1978.

Deleuze, Gilles, *Francis Bacon: Logique de la Sensation,* [Paris], Editions de la Différence ('La Vue le texte'), 1981.

Duckers, Alexander, *Francis Bacon: 'Painting 1946'* Stuttgart, Philipp Reclam jun. ('Werkmonographien zur bildenden Kunst in Reclams Universal-Bibliothek', Nr 145), 1971.

Leiris, Michel, *Francis Bacon face et profil,* Paris, Albin Michel; Munich, Prestel-Verlag; Milan, Rizzoli; Barcelona, Ediciones Poligrafa, 1983, Tr. John Weightman, *Francis Bacon. Full Face and in Profile,* Oxford, Phaidon; New York, Rizzoli, 1983.

Rothenstein, Sir John, *Francis Bacon,* Milan, Fratelli Fabbri Editori, 1963; London, Purnell ('The Masters', 1971); Paris, Hachette, 1967.

Russell, John, *Francis Bacon,* London, Methuen ('Art in Progress'), 1964.

Russell, John, *Francis Bacon,* London, Thames and Hudson, 1971; Paris, Les Éditions du Chêne; Berlin, Prophylaen Verlag. Rev. ed., London, Thames and Hudson; New York, Oxford University Press ('World of Art'), 1979.

Sylvester, David, *Interviews with Francis Bacon,* London, Thames and Hudson; New York, Pantheon Books, 1975. *Samtal med Francis Bacon,* [Stockholm], Forum, [1976]. *Francis Bacon: l'art de l'impossible – entretiens avec David Sylvester,* Preface by Michel Leiris, Geneva, Editions Albert Skira ('Les sentiers de la création'), 1976. *Entrevistas con Francis Bacon,* Barcelona, Ediciones Poligrafa, 1977, Rev.ed., *Interviews with Francis Bacon. 1962-1979,* London, Thames and Hudson, 1980. *Gespräche mit Francis Bacon,* Munich, Prestel-Verlag, 1982.

Trucchi, Lorenza, *Francis Bacon,* Milan, Fratelli Fabbri Editori ('Le grandi monografie: pittori d'oggi'), 1975. Tr. John Shepley, New York, Harry N Abrams, 1975; London, Thames and Hudson, 1976.

Waldegg, Joachim Heusinger von, *Francis Bacon: Schreiender Papst, 1951,* Mannheim, Stadtische Kunsthalle ('Kunst und Dokumentation'), [1980].

## 2 FILMS

*Francis Bacon Paintings 1944-1962,* Samaritan Films (London) for Arts Council and Marlborough Fine Art, dir/scr. David Thompson, 1963.

*Francis Bacon,* Alexandre Burger for Radio Télévision Suisse Romande, dir. Pierre Koralnik, 1964.

*Sunday Night Francis Bacon: Interviews with David Sylvester,* BBC Television, dir. Michael Gill, 1966.

*Francis Bacon,* ORTF; dir. J M Berzosa, interview with Maurice Chapuis, 1971.

*Francis Bacon. Grand Palais 1971,* BBC Television, prod. by Colin Nears, dir. by and interview with Gavin Millar, 1971.

*Sides of Bacon,* London Weekend Television for *Aquarius,* prod. Derek Bailey, dir. Bruce Gowers; incl. interview with David Sylvester, screened 29 Nov 1975 (provinces), 30 Nov 1975 (London).

*Fenêtre sur ... Peintres de notre temps: Francis Bacon,* Antenne 2, prod, Michel Lancelet, dir. Georges Paumier, interview with Michel Lancelet and Edward Behr, screened 19 Apr 1977.

*Après Hiroshima ... Francis Bacon,* Antenne 2 for *Désirs des arts,* presented by Pierre Daix, dir. Pierre Andre-Boutang, interview with Pierre Daix, screened 5 Feb 1984.

*The Brutality of Fact,* BBC Television for *Arena,* dir. Michael Blackwood, prod. Alan Yentob, interview with David Sylvester, screened 16 Nov 1984 (London).

## 3 SELECTED ONE-MAN EXHIBITION CATALOGUES

1962, May-July. London, Tate Gallery, (91 works) introd. by John Rothenstein, text by Ronald Alley.

1962, Oct-Nov. Zürich, Kunsthaus, (78 works) introd. by Sir John Rothenstein, Stephen Spender.

1963, Oct-Jan 1964. New York, Solomon R Guggenheim Museum, (65 works), introd. by Lawrence Alloway. Travelling to Chicago, Art Institute.

1965, Jan-Feb. Hamburg Kunstverein, (61 works), introd. by Ronald Alley.

1965, Feb-Apr. Stockholm, Modern Museet, (63 works.) introd. by Ronald Alley.

1965, Apr-May. Dublin, Municipal Gallery of Modern Art, (57 works).

1971, Oct-Jan 1972. Paris, Grand Palais, (108 works), introd. by Michel Leiris, travelling to Düsseldorf Städtische Kunsthalle (Mar-May 1972)

1975, Mar-June. New York, Metropolitan Museum of Art, (36 works), introd. by Henry Geldzahler, interview with Peter Beard.

1976, July-Sept. Marseilles, Musée Cantini, (16 works), introd. by Gaetan Picon.

1977, Oct-Dec. Mexico, Museo de Arte Moderno, (13 works), introd. by Michel Leris.

1978, Feb. Caracas, Museo de Arte Contemporaneo, (12 works), introd. by Michel Leiris.

1978, Apr-May. Madrid, Fundacion Juan March, (17 works), introd. by Antonio Bonet Correa, travelling to Barcelona, Fundacio Joan Miró (June-July 1978).

1980, Mar-May. Mannheim, Städtische Kunsthalle, text by Joachim Heusinger von Waldegg.

1983, June-Aug. Tokyo, National Museum of Modern Art, (45 works), essay by Masanori Ichikawa, introd. by Sir Lawrence Gowing, travelling to Kyoto (National Museum of Modern Art, Sept-Oct. 1983) and Magoya (Aichi Prefectural Art Gallery, Nov 1983).

1985, May-Aug. London, Tate Gallery, (125 works), essays by Dawn Ades and Andrew Forge, introd. by Alan Bowness.

1988, Sept-Nov. Moscow, Tsentralny Dom Khudozhnika, (22 works) essays by Mikhail Sokolov, introd. by Grey Gowrie.